MONEY DOESN'T GROW ON TREES!

Paul Mason
Illustrated by Mike Gordon

Published in paperback in 2014 by Wayland
Copyright ©Wayland 2014

Wayland
338 Euston Road
London NW1 3BH

Wayland Australia
Level 17/207 Kent Street
Sydney NSW 2000

Editor: Nicola Edwards
Designer: www.rawshock.co.uk

British Library Cataloguing in Publication Data

Mason, Paul
   Money doesn't grow on trees:
   all about managing your money.
   1. Finance, Personal--Juvenile literature.
   I. Title II. Gordon, Mike.
   332'.024-dc22

ISBN: 978 0 7502 8276 5

Printed in China

10 9 8 7 6 5 4 3 2 1

Wayland is a division of Hachette Children's Books,
an Hachette UK company.
www.hachette.co.uk

CONTENTS

MONEY ALL AROUND!

If you want to catch a bus, buy a drink, go to the cinema, or do a thousand other ordinary things, what do you need? Money! Money is all around us, all the time. We use money so often that most of us take it for granted (at least until we run out). But is money as simple as it seems?

Using banknotes instead of chickens or pigs when you wanted to buy something made life a lot easier!

Why was money invented?

Money was invented to make the world an easier place to live in. Before money, people used to exchange goods to get things they needed. They might swap a chicken for some vegetables, for example. For this to work, they had to find someone who had some spare vegetables, and who wanted a chicken.

As soon as money appeared, life became much easier. You could sell your chicken for money, and use the money to buy some vegetables. It was much less bother than the old way! You might even have a bit left over, to save for next week's vegetables.

Early money

It took quite a long time before everyone agreed what money should look like. In China, they used bits of silver as money. On Pacific islands, people used cowrie shells. In New Guinea, it was pigs – try putting one of those in your back pocket when you nip to the shops!

Money today

Today, cash money takes the form of banknotes and coins. Originally these were worth something: a British pound note, for example, could be taken to the Bank of England and swapped for 1lb (450g) of gold. Today, though, banknotes and coins are only valuable because we agree they are.

MONEY MATTERS

¥ $ £ € %

Money worries
Students worry more about their debts than anything else. 59% say debt is their biggest worry, just 29% worry about their studies, and 12% about their social lives.

Money in the bank
Unlike in the olden days, most people no longer keep their money in a box under the bed. Instead, it's usually kept in a bank or savings account. People never get to see all their money together. Instead they get a statement: a printout showing how much money is in each of their accounts.

Managing your money
Managing your money is one of the key skills of modern life. NOT managing your money is a bit like carrying around a bucket of water with holes in it: your money leaks away, bit by bit. However much more you pour in, the bucket never quite gets filled up. Leaking money in this way makes life tougher: shopping expeditions, going to see a live band, and holidays, for example, all become hard to afford.

Fortunately, it's not that tricky to manage your money well. This book is full of tips to help you make sure that as much of your money as possible remains yours – instead of dribbling away!

Confused by money? This book will soon turn on the lightbulb of understanding!

"MONEY'S DULL." Duh! The only time money's dull is when you don't have enough.

HOW MUCH MONEY DO WE NEED?

We all need money — without it, living in the modern world would be impossible. Today, only a tiny number of people could build a home, make clothes, or feed themselves without money. Most of us lack the skills that would be needed. But how much money do we need?

What you need – and what you want

One way to think of your money needs is as a pyramid. The bottom layer is made up of the things you really *need* to survive. The top of the pyramid is made up of things you definitely don't need, but do *want*. Everything else comes somewhere in between.

Things you really don't need (but might like) .... Luxuries such as a new TV (even though the old one isn't actually broken) belong here.

Luxury extras ....

Things that are a good idea .... Holidays, TVs, computer games, a second winter coat, gym membership – these are all things that many people enjoy, but they aren't crucial.

Things that make life more comfortable ....

Most people think it is a good idea to have some savings. That way, if your new bicycle is stolen, your sofa catches fire, or some other unforeseen expense comes up, it won't be a problem.

Things you need to survive ....

Once they have enough money to survive, people usually try to make life a bit better. They might buy more clothes or a bicycle, or donate money to charity, for example.

We all need money to pay for food, clothes, and somewhere to live: without these, it would be impossible for most of us to survive.

The enough-money line

Could you put a ruler across the pyramid to say where a this-is-enough-money line should go? Almost everyone draws the line in a slightly different place. For some people, a simple home and a few possessions are enough. Others feel it is important to own the latest gadgets, a fast car and a big house.

One thing is for sure: the higher up the pyramid you put the line, the more money you will need. Or you can think of it another way: the less money you have, the lower down the pyramid the line HAS to go.

Some people desire nice cars, fancy clothes and the latest mobiles that draw attention to themselves — but lots of others manage happily without them.

MONEY MATTERS

¥　$　£　€　%

"I need more money – my friends can buy more stuff than me."
Don't worry about keeping up with your friends – worry about the things YOU want. If you can't afford them now, turn to page 13 for ideas on how to get the money together.

What money can do for you – and what it can't

There's no doubt that money is very useful stuff – but it can't do everything! These are just a few of the things money can and can't do for you:

Money can:	Money can't:
• Make you feel secure, knowing that even if things go wrong, you will have somewhere to live and food on the table • Make life more comfortable and easier • Get you noticed (maybe because you drive a fancy car, or maybe because you give a lot to charity)	• Make you fit and healthy • Bring you good friends, or love • Make you feel happy or sad if you aren't already

ARE YOU A SPENDER OR A SAVER?

We all have slightly different attitudes to money. Working out what your attitude is will help you manage your money better. If you naturally find it easy (maybe too easy!) to spend money, you will need to think of ways to stop yourself frittering it away. If you find spending money stressful, maybe you need to relax and enjoy it a bit more.

Spending v. saving

We all have to spend money to survive – to get food, clothes and shelter. What you do with any leftover money decides whether you are a spender or a saver. If you spend it on luxuries, without putting any aside, you're a spender – which makes it hard to build up reserves of money for a rainy day.

Case study 1: an extreme spender

Extreme spenders find it hard to keep money in their pockets (or their savings account). Sometimes they show off with money, buying drinks or snacks for everyone else, even if it's not their turn. If extreme spenders see something they want, they buy it. Often they later realize that they didn't really want it at all – if your room is full of things you bought but only played with or wore a few times, you might be an extreme spender.

Which makes you happier: new shoes, or money saved up? The answer will show whether you're a spender or a saver.

Case study 2: an extreme saver

Extreme savers find it hard to spend money, preferring to pile it up in a savings account. You might find them arguing over how much their share of a bill is, or whether they should pay the same as someone else. If you find yourself doing this, or going without things you need even though you can afford them, you might be an extreme saver.

Where do your money habits come from?

Most people get their money habits from their parents. For example, your Mum and/or Dad might be always in a panic about money, wondering how to pay the bills, and not be very good at managing their money. The chances are you'll start off with the same money habits as them.

Getting the balance right

When working out how to manage your money, it is important to get the balance between saving and spending right. Spending every penny, and never knowing quite how you'll pay for things, makes life miserable. But if you *save* every penny, and live in a broken-down old house with peeling wallpaper, life will be miserable too. The trick is knowing how much you need to save, and what you can afford to spend.

He obviously likes to save money — but perhaps this young man could spend some of his money on a new pair of trainers!

MONEY MATTERS

¥ $ £ € %

Money matters: debt mountain

Many people in wealthy countries are increasingly in *debt*. People in the UK have higher personal debts than almost anywhere else. At the start of 2013:

- The amount of personal debt was rising by £164 million – every DAY!
- One person was declared **bankrupt** or insolvent every 5.7 minutes.
- The total personal debt was £1.427 trillion.

Which are you – spender or saver?

This quiz will help you work out if you're a spender or a saver, or somewhere in between. It's important to be honest with your answers! You'll find it easy to work out what the answers 'should' be, if you want to come out as a spender or saver – but what's the point of that?

Striking a balance between spending and saving is the best way to avoid money problems.

1) In your bedroom

Have a look around your bedroom. Which toys or gadgets have you bought (or persuaded someone to buy for you) in the last year? If so, how many times have you used them, on average?

a) Fewer than 10 times
b) Between 10 and 25 times
c) Over 25 times

2) In your wardrobe

Now try the same trick with your wardrobe: look at the new pairs of shoes or items of clothing that have arrived there in the last year (you can leave out school uniform). Work out on average how many times they have been worn:

a) Fewer than 5 times
b) Between 5 and 20 times
c) More than 20 times

3) Stashing your cash

When you're going out for the day with your friends, do you:

a) Automatically take plenty of money with you, because you might see something you want to buy?

b) Take a little bit of money, to buy a drink or some food?

c) Just take enough for the bus fare home: if you need more, you can always come and get it!

4) At the shops

Imagine you're at the shops with your friends. Your best friend buys a new pair of boots, and they look really good. Do you:

a) Buy a pair just like them, right there and then?

b) Decide to think about it, and come back next weekend to see if you still like them?

c) Congratulate your friend on such a good buy (while secretly thinking they were a bit of a waste of money…)?

5) At the end of the week

It's the end of the week, six days since you last got your allowance. What are you thinking?

a) "Oh no – there's none left. And I still haven't paid Tom back from last week. Eek!"

b) "I think I can hear a bit of change jingling in my pocket – but only a bit!"

c) "Nice to see my savings account going up a little bit more this week. Just another £37,862.29 to go until I can afford that Porsche. And the driving lessons, of course…"

Oh dear — no money, no pizza (and no DVDs, new jeans, concert tickets, etc, etc.).

How did you do?

Tot up your answers, and see whether you had mostly a), b) or c).

Mostly a):
You're definitely a spender! Your allowance probably never lasts the week. It would be a good idea to try to stop yourself making impulse buys. Maybe you could decide always to wait a week before buying something you've seen and want?

Mostly b):
Like most people, you're sometimes a spender, and sometimes a saver. You probably always have a bit of money, but not enough to buy something big. It's important that you recognize when it's a good idea to spend money, and when it's better to keep hold of it.

Mostly c):
There's no doubt you're a saver. You're careful about what you spend your money on, and you probably have plenty set aside. Remember, though – it's OK to spend money on things you really want, as long as you can afford them!

GETTING WITH A PLAN

The world is brimful of things to do, and stuff to spend your money on. A new games console, the latest clothes, a skateboard, tickets for the ballet, your favourite football team's kit, presents for your friends, gifts to charities — the list is almost endless! But no one has the time or money to do everything, so how do you decide what you're going to use your money for? The answer is to make a plan!

Dreaming of crucial new stuff?
Make a money plan!

Money plan, stage 1:
What do you want?

The first step towards making a money plan is to decide on what you want to use your money for. A simple example would be if you want to get a new guitar, one that costs £99.99. Making a money plan will help you work out how you can afford it.

Money plan, stage 2:
What do you already have?

The next step is to work out what you already have that can be put towards buying the guitar. Maybe you have £75.00 in a savings account, for example You probably won't want to put all of it towards a guitar – what if tickets for your favourite band come up for sale? But you could decide that a third of your savings can be put towards the guitar.

Money plan, stage 3:
Planning for your goals

You have £25.00 from your savings account, but the guitar costs £100.00. So there's £75.00 to go – where is it going to come from? The next stage of your money plan is to make a list of the places you can get more money to put towards your goals:

Selling off old stuff can be a great way to make a bit of cash. Just make sure you don't get carried away and sell everything off cheap.

• **Allowance**

If you get a regular allowance, say £5.00 a week, you might decide to save half of it towards the guitar. That's £10.83 per month. (Every third month has five weeks in it, not four. To work out a monthly income, multiply the weekly amount by 13 [4 weeks + 4 weeks + 5 weeks = 13], then divide the answer by 3.)

• **Selling stuff**

Perhaps you have some things you could sell? Maybe you could get your Mum or Dad to help you sell your old stuff at a car-boot sale. Old toys, computer games you don't play any more, or books that are too young for you could all earn a bit of money towards the guitar.

• **Earn some money**

Do you have, or could you get, a job? It might not be an 'official' job, like working in a shop. Maybe you could invest in some buckets, sponges and carwash liquid, and start a car-washing business in your street?

Money plan, stage 4: Kerrang!

Once you know how much money is coming in, you can easily work out when you'll be able to afford the guitar:

Savings	£25
Selling old stuff	£14
Allowance	£10.83 a month (2 months = £21.66)
Carwash business	£26 a month (2 months = £52)

Total in 2 months =	£112.66

So inside 2 months, you'll be able to buy yourself the guitar!

DON'T BE A BUDGET MUPPET

Some people drift through life without ever really worrying about money. They spend whatever they like, and don't think too much about how to pay for it. This is **OK** if you're the heiress to a million-dollar fortune. For ordinary people, though, it is a dangerous way of thinking, because it can lead you into debt. Fortunately, there's an easy way to avoid this. It's called a budget.

Income and outgoings

The first step in making yourself a budget is to work out your *income*. Income is the money that comes in, as allowance or earnings. Maybe you get £5.00 a week allowance, and £6.00 a week from your car-wash business. Your income is £11.00 a week, or £47.67 a month.

Next, you need to make a list of your *outgoings*. Outgoings are the things you spend money on. The list might look something like this:

Cinema tickets:	£11 per month (2 visits)
Clothes:	£15 per month (average)
Bus fare to meet friends:	£8 per month
Bike equipment:	£10 per month (average)
Sweets, drinks, etc:	£8 per month
Total:	**£52 per month**

If there's not enough coming in, maybe it's time to think of ways of earning a bit more cash?

If this is what your income and outgoings look like, you're in trouble! There's £47.67 coming in each month – and £52 going out. Not only are you not saving any money, you have a *deficit* of £4.33.

Balancing the budget

When outgoings are more than income, your budget is *unbalanced*. There are only two ways to balance it:
1) Increase your income
2) Decrease your outgoings

In the example above, the only way to increase your income would be to wash more cars. But there are plenty of ways to decrease your outgoings:
• Only go to the cinema once a month
• Buy fewer clothes
• Walk or cycle to meet your friends
• Spend less on your bike
• Kick the sweetie habit

Which of these you choose depends on what's important to you. If you love films, and live a short walk from town, you might give up the bus rides. The important thing is to pick which thing you'll give up – and stick to your decision.

If things go really well, maybe you'll be able to give your friends jobs too. Maybe you'll have to!

MONEY MATTERS

¥ $ £ € %

Money matters: budget tips
Here are some ideas for saving money and making your outgoings smaller:
• Make your own sandwiches instead of buying lunch or snacks.
• Go for a run (free!) instead of going to the pool (costs money).
• Walk or cycle instead of catching the bus.
• Get old clothes altered, instead of buying new ones.

"Don't worry about whether you can afford it now – it'll be OK, we'll sort it out later."
Er – how will it magically get sorted out later? If *you* don't worry about it, who will?

SMART SAVERS ...

One of the reasons for needing to balance your budget (see pages 14 and 15) is so that you don't get into debt. In fact, it is a good idea to try to make your outgoings less than your income, so that there is a bit of money left over each month. That way, you can build up some savings.

Why bother with savings?

There are two main reasons to build up some savings: to make a big purchase, and in case of an unforeseen (and expensive) disaster.

• Buying something big

If you get in the habit of saving, you will have money set aside to pay for big purchases such as a new scooter, mobile phone, etc.

• Unforeseen events

Imagine if, when you are older, your washing machine or TV breaks, or you lose your job. If you have some money saved up, unexpected events like these don't have to be a disaster. You can use your savings to put things right.

Saving is a skill

Some people are better at saving than others. If you have done the quiz on pages 10 and 11, you'll have a good idea of whether you're a saver or spender. If you came out as being a spender, saving money is a skill you will need to work at. The good news is, saving doesn't have to be painful. The 'Money matters' features will give you some ideas of how to start.

If disaster strikes, it's good to have a bit of money put aside to make things right again.

Savings accounts

Most people keep their savings in a savings account. You can open one of these at banks, building societies, or the post office. When you open it, you get a unique account number for paying in and taking out money. You will be sent regular statements, showing how much money is in your account. These usually come either once a month or every three months.

Types of savings account

There are two main types of savings account:

• No-notice accounts

These are accounts where you can take your money out again without warning the bank.

• Notice accounts

With a notice account, you have provide warning (or 'notice') that you want to take the money out.

While your money is being kept by the bank or building society, they pay you a small amount each month for letting them have it. This is called *interest* (see page 26 for more information). You usually get more interest on a notice account than a no-notice account.

You may think it's safely hidden – but really a savings account might be a better place to put your cash.

... AND SAVVY SPENDERS

Even when you are spending money, it's possible to save — by spending less than normal on the things you buy. It does not take much research to find the best prices for the things you need. Lots of people call this getting "good value for money". But is low price the only thing that makes a purchase good value?

What is 'good value'?

Just because something is cheap, that doesn't necessarily mean it is good value. Here are some of the other things you might want to think about when deciding if something is worth buying:

• Will it last a long time?

Is the thing you want to buy well made? A bike that lasts five years is better value than one that falls apart after six months – even if it costs three times as much.

• How long will you want it for?

A pair of purple velvet flares might seem like a good idea now, especially if they are cheap in a sale. But if next month you're embarrassed to wear them, they weren't a good buy.

• Are you paying for the label?

Sometimes you can buy almost the exact-same thing for far less money, but without a fashionable label on it. If it bothers you, just cut the 'unfashionable' labels out when you get home!

Discount vouchers

One way to save money on your shopping is to keep an eye open for discount vouchers. You find these in all kinds of places: on the Internet,

They might be cheap, but that REALLY doesn't mean they're a good idea...

in newspapers, on the packaging for products, even put through your door with free newspapers. (Hint: if your parents don't collect these for things they usually buy, keep them ready for when you go shopping. If you helpfully hand them over at the checkout, maybe you'll get a reward!)

"I got this in the sale – it was half price, so I've saved £15!"
You have – but only if it was something you wanted anyway. If you didn't really need it, you've *spent* £15, not saved it!

Looking for the SALE sign

Sales can be a great place to pick up good value products. You might be able to get jeans or trainers for half price, or even less. The trouble is, it's easy to get carried away and buy things just because they are cheap. But as long as you're buying something you already knew you needed, the SALE sign can point the way to good value.

Shopping around

It usually pays to compare different shops' prices, to find who sells the things you need cheapest. (Remember that Internet sites and catalogues usually charge postage, and if you have to send things back for a different size or colour that may cost money too.)

The 'shopping around' attitude isn't just for things like trainers and DVDs. When you're older, you will be able to apply it to savings and bank accounts, energy supplies, and just about anything else.

MONEY MATTERS

¥ $ £   €   %

Handy hints for spending less
- Never buy anything just because it's cheap.
- Only buy things you really want.
- Never spend money on the spur of the moment.

Sales can be good ways to save money — as long as you buy something you already wanted.

BECOMING INDEPENDENT

In most countries, before you are 18 your parents are partly responsible for your finances. Once you are 18, though, you are usually expected to manage your own money. This is also when many young people get their first job, or study away from home for the first time. So what's involved in managing your own money?

Opening a bank account

If you don't already have one, the first thing you will need to do is open a bank account. This is where any money you are paid will go, and is used to pay your costs. There's advice on what to look for in a bank account and how they work on pages 24 to 25.

"I have a student loan – that must be enough money for everything I need." Whether it's enough or not depends on what you spend. Make a budget to be sure that your money will go far enough to last until the end of term.

Income

When you start work or become a student, you will probably have more money coming in than ever before – whoopee! Don't forget, though: you also have a lot of new outgoings. Some of these are things you will have no choice but to pay, and are called *fixed costs*. Now the budgeting skills you developed in the past (see pages 14 to 15) are really going to come in handy.

When you first start managing your own money, it's very exciting, and can seem like a lot! It soon starts going out again too, though...

Setting a budget

The principles of setting yourself a budget are always the same: your income has to be the same as or more than your outgoings. It's useful to divide your outgoings into two categories: fixed costs (things you have to pay), and variable costs (things you can choose not to pay).

Fixed costs

Fixed costs start with the things at the bottom of the money-needs pyramid on page 6: food, shelter and clothing. You may also now have other fixed costs. If you are a student or training while working, maybe you have to buy paper, pens, books, and other study materials.

When making your budget, start with the fixed costs. The list might look like this:

Accommodation:	£200 per month
Food and drink:	£160 per month
Travel:	£40 per month
Study materials:	£40 per month
Gas and electricity*:	£25 per month

Total:	**£465 per month**

*Don't forget, if you are sharing a house with other people, costs like gas and electricity will be shared.

Variable costs

Variable costs are the things you can choose whether to spend money on. These come from nearer the top of the money-needs pyramid on page 6. They might include guitar lessons, long journeys to visit friends or family, holidays, or sports equipment.

Balancing the budget

Having listed all your outgoings, compare them to your income. It might look like this:

Fixed costs:	£465 per month
Variable costs:	£95 per month

Total:	**£560 per month**

If you have more than £560 per month of income, this is fine. If you have less, you have either to cut your variable costs, or find some way to increase your income.

A bit of sweating in a kitchen might earn you some sweating on the beach!

BANKS AND MONEY

Most of us think of money as cash — notes and coins with which we can buy things. But very few people actually keep all their money in this form. Most of our money is kept in banks. This means our money is kept secure, and makes getting cash or paying bills easy. But unless you manage your bank account carefully, it could be expensive to run.

Banks, in general, are very good at keeping your money safely.

A brief history of banking

The first banks were simply secure places to keep your money and valuables. For doing this, the bankers charged a fee, a bit like a storage charge, which was one of the ways they made money.

Next, banks started to offer their customers a service called a 'note of *credit*'. Instead of buying things with real money, you could hand over your note of credit for, say, a hundred pounds. The seller then took the note of credit to the bank, and was given the hundred pounds. Notes of credit made it possible to do business far away, in places where it would be risky to travel with real money. Of course, the bank charged for issuing notes of credit, so it made a bit of money on each one.

The bankers also realized that they didn't need to have all the money sitting in their bank all the time. They could lend some of it to other people, for which they also charged a fee, like a kind of rental charge on the money. This made them a bit more money.

MONEY MATTERS

  ¥ $ £ € %

Opening a bank account

Rules for opening a bank account depend on the bank and country. In some countries you have to be 18; in others, you can do it at 16. In most places, though, some sort of account is available to young people of 12 years old or more.

If you are able to open an account, you will need to show some official I.D., such as a passport and birth certificate, and prove your address. If you are under 18, one of your parents may have to come along with you, too.

Banking today

Today's banks work in a very similar way to the first banks. People put their money into the bank for safekeeping. The chance of everyone wanting to take out all their money at the same time is tiny, so the bank is able to *invest* some of it, to make more money.

One big difference from the past is that there are lots of new ways to take your money out of the bank (see 'Withdrawals' on page 24). Also, few banks still charge you for storing your money.

Current accounts

Most people keep their everyday money in a type of bank account called a *current account*. This is an account that is designed to allow you to pay in and withdraw money easily. It is not designed for keeping your savings in: for that you need to choose a different type of account (see pages 36 to 39 for more information).

Banks are always keen to sign up new customers, so it's worth shopping around to see who will give you the best welcome.

23

How bank accounts work

Once people have opened a current account, they use it to manage their day-to-day spending. The money they earn is paid in, and the money they spend goes out.

Withdrawals

There are lots of ways to withdraw money or pay bills using your current account, including:

- Use a cash card and *PIN number* to take money out at the cash-point machine.
- Use a debit card and PIN number to make payments.
- Write a cheque, which usually has to be guaranteed with a cheque-guarantee card (often your debit card is also a cheque-guarantee card).
- Transfer money using the Internet, if you have Internet access to your current account.

Paying bills

Many people pay their bills for costs such as accommodation, telephone or heating by cheque. Regular costs such as these can also be paid by standing order or direct debit:

- Standing orders are regular payments of an agreed amount of money. For example, if your rent is £250 per month, you might set up a standing order for £250 per month to your landlord's account. The bank then pays that each month until you tell it not to.
- Direct debits are an agreement to let money be taken from your account for a specific purpose. For example, your phone bill is probably different each month, so it cannot be paid with a standing order. A direct debit allows the phone company to take different amounts each time.

It's important to keep track of the money you pay in to and take out of your bank account.

Paying in

Soon after you open a bank account, the bank sends you a *paying-in book*. To pay in cash or cheques, you visit a branch of the bank, and hand in the money and the filled-in paying-in slip. The cashier tears out the filled-in page, and stamps it and the stub of the torn-out page to prove you have paid the money in.

You might only have overspent by a tiny bit, but the bank could still add surprisingly BIG charges as a result.

Money can also be paid in by computer transfer from another bank. Most large amounts of money, for example wages or student loans, are paid in this way.

The cost of banking

Most banks do not charge you for having a bank account, as long as you have some money. Sometimes, though, a person's bank account goes *overdrawn*. This means he or she has spent more than is in their account, so they owe the bank money. Banks usually charge their customer if this happens.

Some banks charge for sending statements, using cheques and other services. It pays to check what charges a bank could make before you open an account with them.

MONEY MATTERS

¥　$　£　€　%

Understanding your bank statement

Bank statements usually have six pieces of information for each entry:

Date	Description	Details	Money out	Money in	Balance
This tells you the date of the transaction.	This tells you whether money came in/out, and who from/to.	Here you see if it was a cheque, card payment, direct debit, etc.	Sometimes called *debit*, this shows how much money went out.	Sometimes called *credit*, this shows how much money came in.	This tells you how much money was left after the payment in or out.

BORROWING MONEY

Sometimes even people who manage their money carefully find that they don't have enough. Maybe there has been a disaster such as a crashed car that has to be repaired. Or maybe the money is needed to start a business or buy a house, and the cost is too large an amount to save up. In cases like this, many people decide to borrow the money. Borrowing money is often called getting (or taking out) a loan.

How loans work

Loans can come from a variety of places. The most likely place for young people to get loans is from their friends (for small amounts) or their parents (for bigger amounts). Older people can also get loans from banks, building societies, and specialist loan companies.

Usually loans have to be paid back with regular payments over a specific time, for example every month for a year. This is called the *term* of the loan.

Interest

When you borrow money from your friends or parents, you usually only have to pay back the same amount as you borrowed. If you borrow money elsewhere, though, you usually have to pay back a little bit extra. This extra payment is caused *interest*. Charging interest is how banks and other financial organizations make money from loans. Interest is worked out as a percentage of the amount you borrowed. This figure is called the *interest rate*.

MONEY MATTERS

¥ $ £ € %

Loans vs. savings

As well as charging interest on loans, most banks pay interest on your savings. The interest rate charged on loans is always higher than the interest rate paid on savings.

Because you pay more interest on a loan than you earn on savings, it's almost always better to spend your savings than to take out a loan.

Not all loans are the same: those with a higher interest rate are more expensive. There is a guide to working out the interest on a loan on page 29.

Secured and unsecured

There are two main types of loan, secured and unsecured:

• **Secured loans** are ones where the lender gets one of the borrower's possessions if the loan is not repaid. Imagine borrowing £10 from your friend.

He says he wants your bike as *security*. This means if you don't pay the loan back, he gets your bike.

For borrowers, the danger of secured loans is that the amount they borrow (£10) could be less than the value of whatever secures the loan (the bike: £50).

• **Unsecured loans** are ones where the lender has no security if the loan is not repaid. The lender can still try to get the money back, of course, perhaps by taking the borrower to court.

LOANS

Some lenders require you to put up security (something of value), which you lose if you don't pay the loan back. (NB Goldfish, pet dogs and chickens are unlikely to count as security!)

Deciding on a loan

How can you work out if it's a good idea to get a loan or not, and if so which loan you should get? The only way to do this is by finding out the total amount of money you will have to pay back. Ask the lender to tell you exactly how much you will be repaying in total – they will be able to give you a figure.

Interest charges and fees

On most loans, a fixed interest rate is charged. This means that when you agree the loan, both you and the lender know what the interest rate will be. Interest charges on loans are usually worked out on a *compound interest* basis. This means that the longer you have the loan, the more money you pay back as interest. 'Money matters' on page 29 shows how this works.

Some loans (usually *mortgages*, loans for buying a house) have a variable interest rate. The amount of interest you pay changes, depending on whether borrowing money is generally getting more or less expensive.

Banks and other lenders often charge an 'arrangement fee' for setting up a loan. Always check if the lender charges an arrangement fee before taking out a loan.

Paying loans back early

Imagine borrowing money, and then suddenly earning a bit extra that means you don't need the loan any more. You'd like to pay it back.

Paying a loan back early should save you money, because you will be paying interest for a shorter time period. However, some lenders charge you for paying the loan back early: this is called an *early redemption charge*. It is worth checking when you take out a loan whether the lender will make an early redemption charge.

"If I can't afford the repayments over one year, I just make it a two-year loan. That brings the repayments right down." Yes – but it also means you will be paying back far more money in total.

A house is the most expensive thing most of us will ever buy. Mortgage loan repayments are flexible, which means the cost of them can fall or rise.

Lots of people find money management confusing - don't be afraid of asking for help.

MONEY MATTERS

¥ $ £ € %

Compound interest

The cost of most loans is calculated using compound interest. This means that you pay interest not only on the original loan, but also on the interest. Here's a simplified example, for a 3-month loan charging 5% monthly compound interest:

Amount of loan:	Month 1 interest:	Month 2 interest (5% of £105):	Month 3 interest (5% of £110.25):	Total interest paid:
£100.00	£5.00	£5.25	£5.51	£15.76

You can see from this example that the longer you have a compound-interest loan, the more expensive it is.

Look again at the numbers, and something else becomes clear. You would be paying back much more than 5% of the amount you originally borrowed. In fact, you'd be paying 15.76% in three months.

Annual percentage rate (APR)

Because compound interest makes loans complicated, most governments make lenders provide a way for people to compare the cost of loans. This is often called the *annual percentage rate*, or APR. The APR tells you the overall cost of a loan.

CREDIT CARDS: MONEY MUNCHERS

One of the most popular ways for people to borrow money is by using a credit card. Credit cards are a kind of flexible loan. You spend money on the card, and once a month the card company sends you a statement showing how much you have spent. You then pay all or some of the money back. Used carefully, credit cards can be a useful way of paying for things — but they can also be real money munchers.

"Psst! Wanna get a credit card?" It might not seem such a good idea if they were called debt cards!

Expensive borrowing

If you pay off the whole amount due on a credit card each month, no interest is usually charged. But unless the whole amount is paid off, credit cards are an expensive way to borrow money. The card companies usually charge high monthly interest, which means an unpaid debt can quickly grow to an unmanageable size.

Credit cards – or debt cards?

Credit cards could just as well be called debt cards, because they offer you the chance to get into debt. If you only pay back some of the money you have spent on your credit card, the card company carries the rest of the debt over to your next statement. It charges you interest on the carried-over amount.

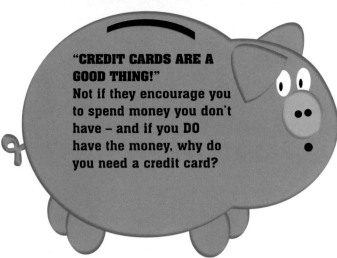

"CREDIT CARDS ARE A GOOD THING!"
Not if they encourage you to spend money you don't have – and if you DO have the money, why do you need a credit card?

People who fall into the minimum payment trap soon find themselves dreading the day on which their credit-card bill arrives.

Each statement lists the amount carried over, this month's spending, and the amount you owe. Unless you owe nothing, there will also be a note saying, 'Minimum payment', and an amount. This is the minimum you have to pay back that month.

The minimum payment trap
Paying off the minimum payment amount on a credit card won't pay off your debt. All it does is give the credit-card company some of your money. The debt still sits there, getting bigger, until your next statement. If all you do is pay off the minimum payment next time, the debt will carry on getting bigger, and bigger, and bigger – and each month, the card company is getting a bit of your money.

Pretty soon, you might find yourself in a situation where all you can afford to pay IS the minimum payment. That's when you're really trapped!

MONEY MATTERS

¥ $ £ € %

Credit vs. debit cards
Credit cards are not the same as debit cards. A debit card is part of your current account. If you spend money on a debit card, the money is taken straight from your current account. Credit cards are separate from your current account, and have their own rules.

TEMPTED TO BORROW

Banks, credit card companies and other financial organizations are keen to lend money, because it's how they make profits. They make borrowing seem as easy and attractive as possible. But just because a loan is good for them, doesn't mean it's good for you. It pays to be aware of some of the language used to get you to borrow money.

Tricks of the (lending) trade

These are some of the ways in which banks, credit-card companies, shops, garages, and other organizations try to attract customers:

Offer: *'Buy now, pay later'*
These are offers where you get to take the goods away immediately, but don't have to pay for them for a long time – often six months or a year later. Sometimes they are advertised as, 'No interest' or, 'Interest free' for a set period of time.

Often found in: Shops selling furniture, electronic goods, and white goods (e.g. washing machines).
Danger: If you do not pay back the whole amount on time, you may be charged interest at a high rate. The interest may be **backdated**, starting from the moment you got the goods.

Offer: *'£100s cashback'*
These are offers where you get some cash back if you buy something or take out a loan. For example, you buy a camera for £350.00 and get £40.00 cashback.
Often found in: Cashback offers are everywhere.
Danger: If someone is offering you cashback, they must be making the cash from the deal in some other way. Probably, either you are paying too much for the goods, or paying too much interest on the loan.

MONEY MATTERS

¥ $ £ € %

Making you feel special

Lenders try to make borrowers feel special and important. They say things like 'You have been specially selected', or tell you about an 'exclusive offer' available only to 'selected customers'. Language like this might make you feel happier about taking out the loan – but it won't help you to repay it!

BE A TOP DOG!

Offer: *Reward schemes*
These are schemes where you are rewarded every time you spend or borrow money. The reward is often in the form of points, which you can 'spend' on products selected by the company.

Often found in: Everywhere, but especially shops and credit-card companies.

Danger: As with cashback, the money for the rewards you are getting has to come from somewhere. The other danger is that you may be tempted to buy a different product from the one you really want, just for the reward.

"Loans are a good idea. After all, they are a way to buy what you want now, and pay for it later! Great!"
Not necessarily. When you take out a loan, you are actually agreeing to pay the lender part of your future income for months or years to come. So you won't be able to enjoy that money later on – which isn't great at all.

It's amazing what people will tell you when they want your money!

GROWING YOUR OWN MONEY

Most people earn money by having a job. But working is not the only way to make money. Once you have some money put aside, you can use it to make more. Using your money to try to make more money is called investing it. Investing is a bit like planting seeds: you plant your money somewhere, and wait for it to grow.

Plant your money in the right place, look after it carefully, and hopefully it will pay you back.

A capital idea

Capital is the name for something – for example, money, property or land – that you can use to earn money. (Income is the name for the money you earn.) When deciding how to invest your money, it is a good idea to keep your capital intact, and only risk changes in your income.

To understand why, imagine a fruit tree. Think of your capital as the tree itself, and the income as the fruit. If you start cutting branches off the tree (i.e. reducing your capital), you will end up getting less fruit next year (i.e. less income).

Making your capital work

Most people use their capital to make money by putting it into a savings account, where it will earn interest. The interest payments are their income. But there are other ways to invest your money:

• Investing in a business

For example, you and your friends might want to start up a business doing bike repairs, or clothes alterations. You would need tools or sewing kit, which cost money. You (or your Mum or Dad) might decide to buy these in return for a share of whatever money the business makes. Be sure it is clear how the investors will get their money out when they want it, though!

• Buying stocks and shares

Stocks and *shares* are a way of investing in big businesses. If you think next year lots of people will be buying bicycles, for example, you might decide to buy shares in a company that makes great bikes.

MONEY MATTERS

¥ $ £ € %

Is money ever bad?

Your money has power. Whether you spend it, let a bank look after it, or invest it yourself, it can be used in various ways:

- Some accounts and investments might use your money to pay for manufacturing weapons, slave labour, and polluting industries, for example. These may be profitable, but some people would prefer that their money wasn't used in this way.
- Other accounts and investments make promises about how your money will be used. They may invest in renewable technology, organic farming, or fair-trade industries, for example. Some people prefer to know their money is being used in this way.

Earning money doesn't have to be dull or boring! Maybe you're good at making people laugh, or clowning around, and someone will pay you to do it.

RISKS AND REWARDS

People who want to invest their money have to ask themselves one very important question: 'How much risk am I willing to take?' The answer to this question depends on whether you can afford to lose some or all of the money. It also decides how much of a reward you could get for your investment.

A day at the races

Investing money is a bit like betting on a horse race. Imagine you're at the racetrack, and there's a horse that is almost certain to win. There are only two other horses in the race, one of them fat and the other old. Placing a bet on the young, slim horse is not likely to win you much money. In the investment world, near-certain winners like this are called a *safe* or *low-risk investment*.

The other extreme is to bet on the fat horse, or maybe the old one. No one expects either to cross the line first.

Betting on one of these could win you a lot of money! But there's also a big risk that you will *lose* everything. This is a *high-risk investment*.

Low risk, low reward

If you were down to your last pound coin, you probably wouldn't bet it on the fat horse or the old one. You'd rather be almost certain of winning a small amount than risk having nothing left. Investments work in the same way: if you cannot afford to lose your money, you need a safe or low-risk investment.

Regardless of which horse wins this race, you wouldn't bet on any of them unless you didn't mind losing your money.

High risk, high reward?

Now imagine you have £7.00 in your pocket, and you get your allowance tomorrow. You might feel willing to risk a pound on one of the high-risk horses. It won't really matter if you lose. Investing works the same way: if you can afford to lose some or all your money, you *could* choose a high-risk investment.

Making the right investment can be like backing a winning horse - but investing money, like gambling, is a risky business.

MONEY MATTERS

¥ $ £   €   %

Deciding on an investment

Once you have decided on the level of risk you are willing to take, and what kind of investment you need, these are some other things to consider:

- **How do I get my money out?**
  With some investments you have to give warning that you want your money back. Some savings accounts, for example, work in this way. You might have to let them know a month, three months or even a year in advance. It might be impossible to get your money back sooner, or you may *forfeit* some or all of the interest you would have earned.

- **How long can I leave the money there?**
  The value of many investments goes up and down. Imagine you have bought shares in a company, or a piece of Banksy artwork. In six months' time, they might be worth less than you paid for them. If you *had* to sell in six months, you would lose out. If you could afford to wait until prices rose again, it might still turn out to have been a good investment.

"I've found an investment that guarantees an unbelievable profit really quickly. I'm going to invest." If it seems too good to be true, it usually is. Read the small print of the deal very carefully: big profits almost never come with cast-iron guarantees.

Diversification

Diversification is the name for spreading your investments around. Investing your money in several different places makes it less likely that you could lose some or all of it. If all your money were invested in one place, it would be disastrous if that investment crashed in value. But if you split your money between four investments, one of them crashing is less serious.

A balanced portfolio

A group of investments is sometimes called a *portfolio*. Most investors aim to have a balanced portfolio. This means that they have a variety of investments, of different types and levels of risk. Imagine dividing your money in four:

• Quarter could go into a nice, safe savings account where you can get at it straight away

• Quarter could go into a long-notice savings account, which pays a higher rate of interest

• Quarter could be invested in shares

• Quarter could be spent on a piece of Banksy artwork, a rare vinyl album, or something else you think might increase in value

A portfolio like this would have a good balance between security and risk.

Some people choose to invest their money in art, or other objects they are interested in.

Money matters: judging your investment

How do you decide what kind of investment to make? Start by judging whether you can afford to lose some or all of your capital (the money you invest). The chart opposite will then help you decide where you could put your money:

Investment:	Typical risk:	Possible reward:	Investment level:
Savings account	Almost none: even if the bank fails, most governments guarantee to refund your savings.	Relatively low interest rates.	One of the safest places to put your money: up to 100% of it could go into savings accounts.
Stocks and shares	Because any business can fail, it is possible you could lose some, or even all, of your money.	The value of your shares *could* rise dramatically. You may also be paid a *dividend* if the company makes enough money.	Because the risk is higher, it would be unwise to invest more than you can afford to lose.
Investment funds	Investment funds buy shares in a variety of companies, so even if one goes bust, the others will still be there. This spreads the risk.	With less risk comes less reward. Also, the fund's managers will expect to be paid before you get your share.	Although your money is safer than in individual stocks and shares, its value can still go down. Make sure you have enough savings elsewhere to cover most of your needs.
Investing in art, antiques, etc.	The risk depends on how much you know about the subject. Would you be able to spot a Rembrandt at a garage sale? If so, the risk in buying it would be low.	The reward also depends on you. If you thought it was a Rembrandt and it turned out not to be, you would have lost your money.	Only spend what you can afford to lose – unless you're 100% sure it is a Rembrandt.
Property	Most people buy property using a loan called a *mortgage*. If the value of the property falls, you can be left owing more money than the property is worth.	After many years you will have paid back the mortgage and will own the property. If it is your home, your housing costs will then be small.	Always make sure you can afford the mortgage repayments.

TAX AND INFLATION

However good you are at money management, there are two things affecting your money that you cannot control. The first is taxes, and the second is inflation. Each of these makes a real difference to both your earnings and your savings — and rarely in a good way.

What is tax?

Tax is a way of the government getting money. The money is then spent on things the government provides for it citizens. For example, tax money may be used to pay for our schools, armed forces, and healthcare.

The government gets tax money by taking a percentage of almost every financial exchange. For example, if you earn £1500.00 a month, the government might take 20% of it (or £300.00) as tax. This type of tax is called *income tax*, but there are many other kinds. For example:

- Sales tax is added to the cost of goods. If you buy a pen for 99p, for example, about 20p of that goes to the government.

Don't let your money slip away this easily!

- Death taxes are charged when someone dies. The government takes a percentage of their money before it is handed on to the dead person's heirs.

- Property taxes are charged to people who own a property. They are usually based on the value or size of the property.

What is inflation?

Inflation is the name for the way that prices go up over time. For example, if a steak cost £5.00 a year ago, but costs £5.50 today, its price has undergone inflation. Inflation is usually shown as a percentage. In the example, steak inflation is running at 10% a year, because the 50p increase is 10% of the old £5.00 price.

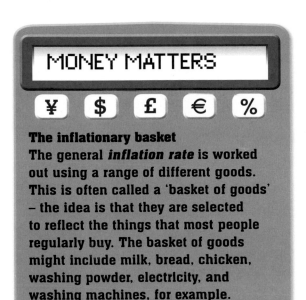

MONEY MATTERS

¥ $ £ € %

The inflationary basket

The general *inflation rate* is worked out using a range of different goods. This is often called a 'basket of goods' – the idea is that they are selected to reflect the things that most people regularly buy. The basket of goods might include milk, bread, chicken, washing powder, electricity, and washing machines, for example.

Inflation rates are based on the changing cost of an imaginary 'basket of goods'.

How does inflation affect your money?

Inflation affects your money in two main areas: earnings, and savings and investments:

Earnings

Inflation affects your earnings because, over time, it makes them worth less. Imagine you earn £25,000 a year, and are given a pay rise. Sounds good – but is it? You won't know without taking inflation into account:

Old salary:	New salary (with 5% pay rise):	Inflation at 3% of old salary:
£25, 000	£26, 250	£750

A 5% pay rise means you earn £1250 extra each year. If inflation is at 3%, you need to earn 3% more – £750 – to be able to afford the same things as last year. So your pay rise is *really* worth £500 (the extra £1250 minus £750).

Savings and investments

Inflation affects savings and investments in the same way as earnings. For example, you might earn 3% interest on your savings account. But if inflation is at 3% as well, the value of your money isn't really increasing, it is just staying the same.

THE P WORD – PENSIONS

If you hear someone say 'pensions', what do you think of (just before your eyes start to glaze over and you nod off to sleep)? Delete if appropriate: grey hair, false teeth, going bald, trousers with elastic waistbands, all-you-can-eat lunches, Saga holidays.

Doesn't look retired... doesn't look old enough — but with a bit of financial planning, perhaps you too could be free to ski into your 50s.

Fortunately, it doesn't have to be that way! How about this: waking up whatever time you like, going out for a coffee at 11, late lunch, then staying up till 2.30 a.m. because that one Steven Seagal movie you haven't yet seen is on Channel 5? Maybe you'll go snowboarding for a month in the winter, travel round Europe in your campervan in the summer, and get cheap flights everywhere because you can travel on a Wednesday morning?

To do this young enough to enjoy it, though, you need to think about a pension **RIGHT NOW**. Otherwise, you'll probably still be clocking on at B&Q four days a week at 75 years old.

What is a pension?

A pension is a scheme for providing people with income after they have stopped working. Usually they can only collect their pension payments when they get to a specific age. Some pensions reward people who put off, or defer, collecting their pensions until a later age.

How do pensions work?

Pensions work by collecting money from people who are working, in order to be able to pay out money in the future, when they have stopped working. The two main types of pension are state pensions and private pensions.

State pensions

In some countries, the government provides everyone with a small pension. The money is collected from working people's taxes. Most people are happy to pay in, knowing it means they get money out when they are older. State pensions provide enough money for basic survival, but little more.

Imagine the fun you'll have later if you start saving now.

Private pensions

Many people choose to be part of a private pension scheme. In this, they pay into a fund that is invested for them, which hopefully means their fund will grow. When they retire, the fund is used to provide a regular payment of money each month.

"I don't need to worry about pensions now – I'll think about that when I'm old."
The trouble with that is, when you are old it will be too late. The sooner you start planning your pension, the more fun you will be able to have when you are older. Of course, that doesn't mean you can't have fun now as well!

Self-planned pensions

Some people prefer to plan their own pension. For example, they might buy a second home, and aim to pay off the mortgage before they retire. The home can then be rented out, providing them with an income.

TEST YOUR MONEY SKILLS

Having read this book, you probably understand more about the world of money and how it works than before. But how much has really sunk in? Run through our money-skills quiz to find out! (Note your answers on a sheet of paper, and check whether you were correct at the bottom of page 47.)

1) Why were bank notes first invented?
   a) So that money could be folded up and put in a wallet or purse.
   b) To help people trade safely in distant places.
   c) It gave the government a chance to put pictures of politicians on our money.

2) We all need money. But what decides the minimum amount you need each month?
   a) The rise or fall in the costs of new games for your Wii.
   b) The cost of food, clothing and somewhere to live.
   c) Whether or not Christmas is coming up and you have lots of presents to buy.

3) Which of these things can money get you?
   a) A fancy-looking convertible car.
   b) A big house with a swimming pool.
   c) Good friends.

4) How much money is enough?
   a) The same amount as my friends have.
   b) A little bit more than my friends.
   c) Enough to cover my own needs.

5) Where do most people learn their attitude to money?
   a) Their parents.
   b) Their teachers.
   c) Their friends.

6) You unexpectedly get given £100. What should you do with it?
   a) Spend it! After all, you weren't expecting it, so it's not 'real' money, is it?
   b) Put it all straight in your savings account and forget about it.
   c) It depends: if you already have some money saved up, and there's something you've been wanting to buy yourself for ages, then spend it. If you've just had to spend all your savings, because your bike was stolen, save it.

7) What is a money plan?
   a) A list of things you want to buy.
   b) A design for a new bank note.
   c) A way of working out how you can afford to buy something.

8) A budget is a way of working out if you have enough money coming in to cover your expenses. When your budget is unbalanced, what does it mean?
   a) You haven't spent all your money.
   b) Your spending is higher than your earnings.
   c) Your budget is a bit loony.

9) What's a good way to save money painlessly?
   a) Put 10% of everything you earn into a savings account.

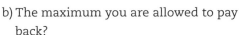

b) Give something up and put the money you save into your savings account.

c) Both of the above.

10) When is it a good idea to buy things in a sale?

a) When something you already wanted is on special offer.

b) Whenever you spot a real bargain, with loads of money off.

c) If you see something you think will be useful, even if you've never heard of it before.

11) What type of bank account do most people keep their money in?

a) A current account.

b) A raisin account.

c) An I-can't-count.

12) Is a standing order:

a) When an Army officer tells you not to sit down?

b) A way to pay the same amount of money out of a bank account regularly?

13) What is a 'term'?

a) The time in between school holidays.

b) The time in which you pay back a loan.

c) Both of the above.

14) Are interest rates:

a) Ways of showing how good the audience thought a movie was?

b) A measure of how much a lender will charge you to borrow money?

15) Is the 'minimum payment' on a credit card:

a) The minimum you have to spend next month to keep the card going?

b) The maximum you are allowed to pay back?

c) The minimum you have to pay back this month (and a good way for the credit-card company to earn interest)?

16) You get a letter from a company offering to lend you money. It says you've been 'specially selected' for a 'pre-approved loan'. Do you think:

a) 'Wow! What luck! These sound like people I'd like to borrow money from.'

b) 'Hmm – me and everyone else from my postal district, you mean. No thanks.'

17) What is capital?

a) The city where a country's government is based.

b) Something (usually money) that earns you income.

c) An old-fashioned way of saying 'Good idea!'

18) What should help you decide whether or not to take on a risky investment?

a) Whether you're feeling lucky that day.

b) How much you will earn if it pays off.

c) Whether or not you can afford to lose the money.

19) In the money world, inflation is a word for describing:

a) Blowing up balloons, ready for the bank's Christmas party.

b) How much prices have increased.

20) Is a pension:

a) A place to stay when on holiday in France (look up *pension* in a French dictionary)?

b) A plan for having some income when you stop working?

GLOSSARY

annual percentage rate (APR)
number that tells you the overall cost of a loan each year

bankrupt
officially without enough money to pay off debts

compound interest
loan interest that is paid not only on the original amount borrowed, but also on the amount of interest charged

credit
payment in, or amount of money above zero

current account
bank account used for paying money in and out during day-to-day money transactions

debit
payment out, or amount of money below zero

debt
amount of money owed

deficit
shortfall, caused by spending more money than you have

dividend
payment made to shareholders in a company or business, if that business makes profits

early redemption charge
amount of money charged by some lenders for paying a loan back early

fixed costs
costs that cannot be avoided, and which do not change

forfeit
give up or surrender

high-risk investment
investment that offers a good chance that you will lose some or all of the money you've put in

income
money that is paid to you from e.g. earnings, savings or investments

income tax
percentage of the money you earn that has to be paid to the government

inflation rate
amount by which the cost of goods and services increases, given as a percentage

interest
amount of money paid on credit in current and savings accounts, given as a percentage

interest rate
number describing the amount of interest paid, given as a percentage

invest
put money into something, in the hope of getting more money back

low-risk investment
investment that offers only a small chance that you will lose some or all of the money you've put in

mortgage
loan for buying a house. If the loan repayments are not made, the lender gets the house

outgoings
things you spend money on

overdrawn
having a sum in your bank account that is below zero

pension
regular payment of money after you have reached a certain age (usually between 60 and 75)

PIN number
short for Personal Identification Number, a number known only

FURTHER INFORMATION

to the holder of a bank account, which is used when withdrawing money and making payments

portfolio
group or set of investments

profit
income from a financial deal, exceeding the amount invested

safe investment
investment in which there is no chance that you will lose any of the money you have put in

security
in money circles, something that makes it safe to lend someone money, and which the borrower will lose if they do not repay the loan

stocks and shares
investments in businesses. If the business is profitable, the stock-holders will be paid part of the profit. Stock is usually divided into small fractions, which are called stocks or, more often, shares

statement
table showing how much money has gone into and out of a financial account

BOOKS

Show Me The Money Alvin Hall (Dorling Kindersley, 2008)
A great guide to all things money, by the Guru of sensible attitudes to money, Alvin Hall. The book is easy to dip into, and as always uses good, clear examples and gives very practical advice.

The Teenager's Guide To Money Jonathan Self (Quercus Publishing, 2007)
A clear, entertaining read, this book gives practical advice and information on a range of money-related topics. In particular it's good on budgeting, coping with money at college, and how bank accounts work.

I'm Broke! The Money Handbook Liam Croke (ticktock Media, 2009)
A light-hearted, but useful, guide to world of personal finance, full of information, advice and tips.

Life Skills: Raising Money and Managing Money Barbara Hollander (Heinemann Library, 2008)
Advice on getting, using and saving money, with real-life examples.

A Young Citizen's Guide To Money Anna Davidson (Wayland, 2002)
Contains useful and interesting information on the history of money; how banks, building societies and other financial organizations work; and personal finance.

WEBSITES

http://www.moneysavingexpert.com/family/Teenagers-cash-class
Download a really useful and comprehensive guide to savvy money management from money saving expert Martin Lewis.

http://www.guardian.co.uk/money/2007/nov/22/personalfinancenews
Top money saving tips for teens from Jonathan Self, author of *The Teenager's Guide to Money*.

http://www.fool.com/teens/teens02.htm
This US-based site offers plenty of useful information and tips on a range of money-related topics.

ANSWERS TO THE QUIZ ON PAGES 44-45:

1) b; 2) b; 3) a and b; 4) c; 5) a; 6) c; 7)c; 8) b; 9) c; 10) a; 11) a; 12) b; 13) c; 14) b; 15) c; 16) b; 17) b, 18) c; 19) b; 20)a and b

INDEX